THE MIDDLE AGES

Peter Chrisp

Come and explore **MY WORLD** and find out what it's like to live in the Middle Ages.

Hello, I'm Robin

I'm called Isobel

My name is Tom

TWO CAN™

PRINCETON ■ LONDON

www.two-canpublishing.com

Published in the United States and Canada by
Two-Can Publishing LLC
234 Nassau Street
Princeton, NJ 08542

© 2002, 1997 Two-Can Publishing

For information on Two-Can books and multimedia,
call 1-609-921-6700, fax 1-609-921-3349, or visit our website at
http://www.two-canpublishing.com

Art direction and design Helen McDonagh
Editor Claire Watts
Consultant Judy Stevenson BA, Dip. Mus. Stud., Museum of London
Managing Editor Christine Morley
Managing Art Director Carole Orbell
Cover design Helen Holmes
Model maker Melanie Williams
Illustrator David Hitch
Photography John Englefield

'Two-Can' is a trademark of Two-Can Publishing.
Two-Can Publishing is a division of Zenith Entertainment Ltd,
43-45 Dorset Street, London W1U 7NA

HC ISBN 1-58728-063-9
SC ISBN 1-58728-069-8

HC 1 2 3 4 5 6 7 8 9 10 04 03 02
SC 1 2 3 4 5 6 7 8 9 10 04 03 02

Printed in Hong Kong by Wing King Tong

CONTENTS

Me and my world

My name's Robin and I'm nine years old. I live in a village in the county of Suffolk in the east of England. It's the year 1250 and King Henry III is the ruler of England.

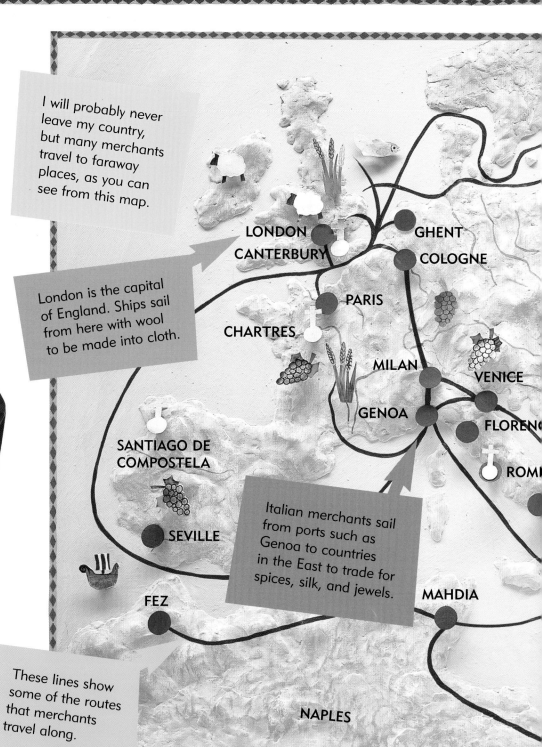

I will probably never leave my country, but many merchants travel to faraway places, as you can see from this map.

London is the capital of England. Ships sail from here with wool to be made into cloth.

Italian merchants sail from ports such as Genoa to countries in the East to trade for spices, silk, and jewels.

These lines show some of the routes that merchants travel along.

LONDON
CANTERBURY
GHENT
COLOGNE
PARIS
CHARTRES
MILAN
VENICE
GENOA
FLORENC
SANTIAGO DE COMPOSTELA
ROM
SEVILLE
FEZ
MAHDIA
NAPLES

Signs on the map

Important towns	Religious centers	Wool	Wine	Grain
Fur	Fish	Honey		

Wool, wine, grain, fur, fish, and honey are some of the important goods that countries trade with each other.

My country

Most English people live, like me, in the countryside. There are also towns where merchants and craftspeople live. The greatest place of all is London, which is an important port. Ships from London sail to such places as Italy and France with wool, grain, and cheese. They return with wine, cloth, spices, and furs.

Traveling abroad

It is difficult and expensive to travel. This is why most people, apart from merchants, rarely journey farther than the nearest town. Some people go on a pilgrimage if they have money or are religious. This is a journey to a holy place, such as the burial site of a saint. The most important pilgrimage is to the land where Jesus Christ lived. We call this place the Holy Land.

NOVGOROD

CONSTANTINOPLE

ANTIOCH

JERUSALEM

This is the Holy Land. Some people journey here for religious reasons.

CAIRO

My family

I live with my mother, my father, and my brother, Tom, who's ten. We are poor farmers who work and live on land that belongs to a rich man called a lord. He lets us grow food for ourselves, but in return, we must do his work.

Father and Mother

Father is an important man in our village. He is the reeve, the man chosen by all the villagers to be in charge of the farming. He decides when to plant the crops and when to harvest them. Mother looks after our house, cooks our meals, and makes our clothes. At busy times of the year, such as harvesttime, she also works in the fields.

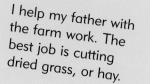

This is my brother, Tom. He is getting ready to go on a trip to London.

I help my father with the farm work. The best job is cutting dried grass, or hay.

Lords and villeins

All of my family, like many others in the village, are villeins. This means that we cannot do anything without first asking the lord. Tom wants to work in London when he's older, but he can only go if the lord lets him.

The steward's daughter

My friend Isobel is the daughter of the steward, who makes sure all the farm work is done for the lord. The steward is richer than everyone else in the village because the lord pays him good wages. Isobel and her family live in the biggest house in the village. It doesn't belong to them, though. It is owned by the lord, who lives in a castle a day's cart ride from the village.

Playtime

When Tom and I have finished helping with the farm work, we play with Isobel and our other friends. In the summer, we play soccer, and in the winter, when the pond freezes over, we go ice-skating on skates made out of wood or bone.

These toy soldiers belong to Isobel. She has some nice toys that her father has bought for her.

Let's make a toy soldier

✳ Adult help needed

Find cardboard, a pencil, scissors, paints, a paintbrush, felt-tip pens, 4 two-pronged paper fasteners, and glue.

1 Cut out the shapes shown here from the cardboard.

2 Paint both sides of the shapes to look like a soldier. Draw the face and armor with felt-tip pens.

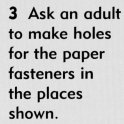

3 Ask an adult to make holes for the paper fasteners in the places shown.

4 Attach the arms, legs, and handle to the body with the fasteners. Now glue the shield on the body.

Our home

We live in a small, one-room cottage that's warm and cozy. In the garden, my mother grows vegetables and herbs for us to eat. Our chickens, geese, and pigs live in the garden too. We have everything we need, except water, which I carry from the well daily.

Wattle and daub

Father built our cottage when Tom was a baby. First, he made a wooden frame, which he filled in with strips of hazel wood called wattle. He plastered the walls with daub, a mixture of straw, mud, and dung. Lastly, he made a straw roof, called a thatch.

It's hard work carrying these buckets when they're full!

Our windows are covered with canvas to keep out drafts.

My mother grows some vegetables to sell at the market.

There is no kitchen in our home. Food is stored in sacks and baskets. Fresh meat and herbs are hung up to dry.

Inside our cottage

The floor of our cottage is made of dirt that is packed down to make it hard. In the middle of the room, we have a fire burning to give us warmth and light and to cook our food. We use candles for light too. The candles are made from animal fat. We don't have much furniture, just a table, some stools, and a wooden chest for our belongings. We sleep on mattresses filled with straw.

The pigs live in a pen in the yard. It's my job to feed them scraps every day.

Our village

About 80 people live in our village, and some of them are related to me. My father's parents and my two uncles and their families live here, but my mother's family lives in another village. I know all the people in the village because we work together in the fields. One of my jobs is to scare birds from the fields with stones thrown from my sling.

If I hit a starling or a crow, Mother will put it in a pot and cook it.

In your time...
For hundreds of years, people farmed in huge fields divided into small plots or strips. In some places, you can still see the patterns left on the land by these fields.

The church is the tallest building in the village. It's made of stone.

This is the manor house, where Isobel and her family live.

Our fields

Beside our village, there are three big fields where we grow crops, such as wheat, barley, rye, oats, beans, and peas. Each year, two fields are planted with crops. Part of each field is used for growing food for the lord, and the rest is divided into strips. Every family has a number of strips in each field. We have 15 strips of land. The third field is left unplanted, which allows nutrients to return to the soil.

Sharing the work

In the autumn, the villagers plow one of the fields and sow wheat or rye. In the spring, they plow the second field and sow a different crop. Summer begins with haymaking. Everyone joins in, cutting and gathering the hay in the meadow, which will be fed to the animals in the winter. Then, in late summer, the sheep are sheared and the crops that have been growing in the fields are harvested.

We are halfway through plowing this field.

This field has only weeds growing in it. Next year, we will plant crops here.

We have to pay the lord to have our wheat ground into flour at his mill.

Our lord

Last week, Father and I went to the lord's castle to deliver flour and peas for his kitchen. My father and the other men from our village go to the castle about once a month to make deliveries or help with work on the land around the castle. Whenever the lord sends for us and tells us to do something, we have to obey him. We can't even marry or leave our village without his permission.

The language of the nobles

Rich people, such as the lord and lady, are called nobles. Most nobles speak French and can hardly understand a word of English. We villeins speak English, although my father knows the French words for crops and animals. Isobel's father can speak both languages.

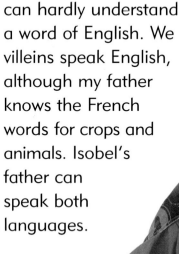

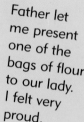

Father let me present one of the bags of flour to our lady. I felt very proud.

Serving the king

Most land in England belongs to the king. But a long time ago, the king gave the nobles the right to use the land to build castles and villages like ours. In return, the nobles have to follow the king into battle. They must provide foot soldiers and knights, or they must give money to help pay for the soldiers and knights.

The great castle

The castle is a strong stone building, protected from almost any attack. It is home to the lord, his family, his followers, and servants. The castle is like a little village, with everything the lord needs, including a huge storeroom, a chapel, and a dungeon.

The top floor is used only by the lord's family. They sleep there and also spend time there when they have no guests.

The great hall is the castle's main room. It's where the lord holds feasts.

Prisoners are taken through this door down to the dungeon.

13

While we were at the castle, Father and I saw a tournament. This is a pretend battle fought between knights. I waved a flag to show which knight I supported.

A suit of iron

To protect himself from injury, each knight is covered from head to foot in a coat of iron rings called chain mail. Over this, he wears a wool garment called a surcoat. He carries a wooden shield and wears a strong helmet.

Coat of arms

Each knight's shield is decorated with a picture or pattern called a coat of arms. His cloak is decorated in matching colors. This helps the knights recognize each other, even when their faces are covered by their helmets.

A knight uses a long pole called a lance to knock his opponent off his horse.

In your time...

In many sports today, teams wear their own special colors. Their supporters wear shirts or scarves in the same colors too.

Charge!

The knights charge at each other on horses. The aim is to knock a rival knight off his horse using a lance. It's very dangerous!

The Crusades

Many knights go to the Holy Land to fight the Muslims in a war called a crusade. The Muslims rule much of the Holy Land, and they belong to a religion that is different from ours. The crusaders think that people of our religion, called Christians, should rule the Holy Land.

The horse is covered with cloth to match the knight's colors.

Let's make a shield

Find thick cardboard, scissors, a ruler, a pencil, a paintbrush, paints, and tape.

1 Cut out a cardboard shield, about 20 inches x 14 inches (50 centimeters x 35 centimeters).

2 Draw a coat of arms on your shield. You could draw a pattern or a shape, such as a star or a flower. Paint your design and leave it to dry.

3 Cut out a 14-inch (35-cm) handle and tape it to the back of the shield. Hold it up by putting your arm under the handle.

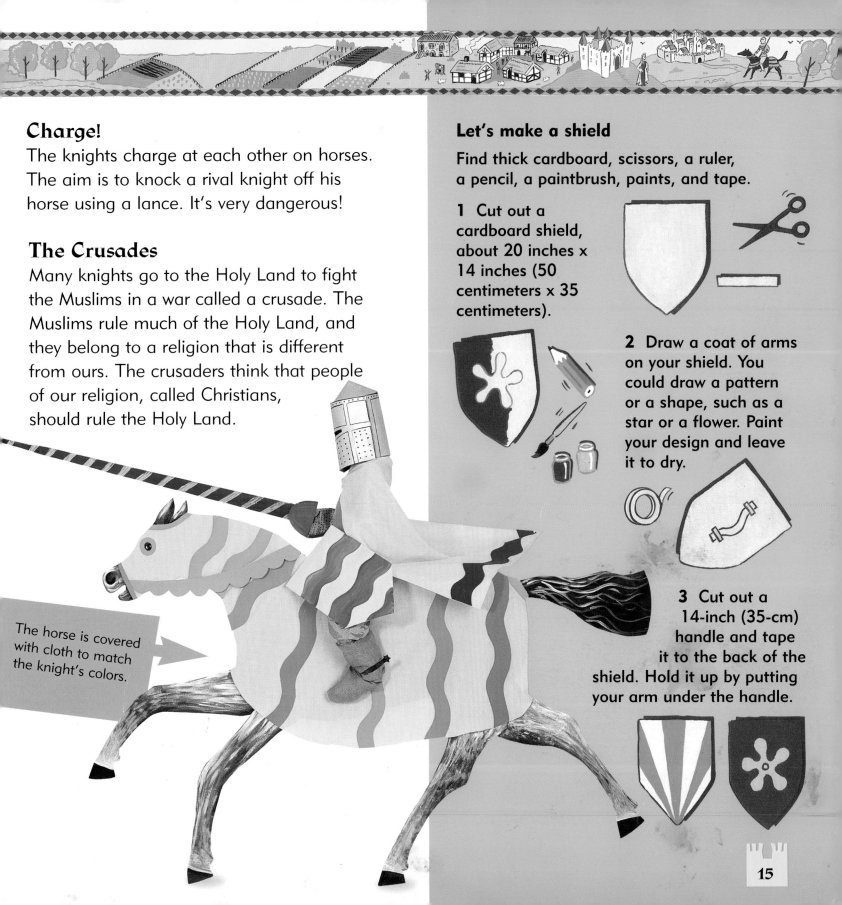

15

Only nobles are allowed to keep hawks like this for hunting.

Isobel and I have been dressing up today. She's dressed like a peasant woman and I'm wearing the kind of clothes a lord would wear. Poor villeins like me don't usually wear fine clothes, like this fur-trimmed robe and jeweled brooch.

Let's make a brooch

★ Adult help needed

Find stiff cardboard; scissors; a toothpick; self-hardening clay; gold, red, and blue paint; a paintbrush; glue; and tape.

1 Cut out a ring of cardboard 3 inches (7 cm) across. Shorten the toothpick to 2 ½ inches (6.5 cm).

2 Make eight small clay balls and let them dry out. Paint the balls gold, red, and blue. Paint the ring and toothpick gold.

My robe is trimmed with fur called sable.

Fine clothes for the rich

The lord and lady dress in soft materials, such as silk and linen, and bright colors, including scarlet, blue, and green. They wear long, loose robes. When it's cold, they wrap themselves in warm cloaks lined with fur.

Homemade clothes

My mother makes most of my clothes from wool that she spins herself. I wear stockings called hose and a shirt and tunic on top. In cold weather, I wear a wool cap to keep my ears warm. Women wear long, loose dresses and usually keep their hair covered with a piece of cloth.

Isobel is wearing a big apron to keep her dress clean while she collects hens' eggs.

3 Glue the balls to the brooch and let the glue dry.

4 Glue and tape the toothpick to the back of the brooch. Ask an adult to attach the brooch to your clothes by threading the toothpick through a buttonhole.

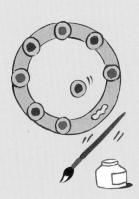

Precious jewels

Lords and ladies sometimes fasten their clothes with gold brooches. They wear other jewelry too, such as gold rings on their fingers.

Rich people often wear brooches like this to show everyone how wealthy they are.

Mother made this bread from wheat grown on our land. We eat the same type of food every day, but there's always plenty of it. Rich people eat all kinds of delicious foods, such as the sweet, spiced honey toasts I tasted once at Isobel's house.

Rye is mixed with wheat to give the bread a nutty flavor.

Feeding our family

For supper, we usually have a thick stew made with beans, peas, and other vegetables and perhaps some fish or rabbit. In winter, we kill a pig and smoke it over the fire to preserve it. The meat will last us nearly all winter. For other meals, we have bread with ewe's cheese that Mother makes.

Let's make honey toasts

Adult help needed

Find a saucepan; a wooden spoon; ½ cup (225 grams) honey; pinch each of ground ginger, cinnamon, ground pepper; two slices of bread; and some pine nuts.

1 Put the honey and spices in a saucepan. Ask an adult to put the pan on a low heat and stir for two minutes.

2 Toast the bread lightly on both sides. Now stick the pine nuts in each piece.

3 Ask an adult to pour the honey mixture over the toast and serve immediately.

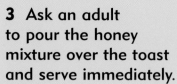

A feast at the castle

My friend Isobel went to a feast at the castle. There were dozens of dishes, including a roast boar and a blackbird pie. Many dishes were made with spices from foreign lands, and there were fruits I've never tasted, such as figs and grapes. The guests used slices of thick, stale bread as plates. These plates, called trenchers, were given to poor people to eat afterwards.

Eating meat

Our priest says that we shouldn't eat meat on Wednesdays, Fridays, Saturdays, and for 40 days before Easter. On these days, people must eat fish instead. But since we villagers don't often eat meat, it doesn't make much difference to us.

Water is too dirty to drink, so rich people drink wine.

The lord is eating a tiny bird called a quail that has been cooked on a skewer.

When this lady has finished eating, she'll throw the bones on the floor for the dogs.

Life isn't all hard work in our village. No one works on Sundays or on festival days, called holy days. Every week, a market is held in our local town. There are lots of things to buy and entertainers to watch. I like the jugglers best. I'm learning to juggle, but it's not easy!

In your time...
The word "holiday" comes from "holy day," the name for a church festival in the Middle Ages.

Buying and selling

People come to the market from nearby villages to sell wool, grain, or animals and to buy goods, such as cloth and new tools. I love watching the entertainers. There are acrobats, who throw themselves through the air, trained dogs that can walk on their hind legs, and sometimes actors performing plays.

Let's make juggling balls

Find colored fabric, needle, thread, and rice.

1 For each ball, cut out four pieces of fabric 5 inches x 2 inches (12 cm x 5 cm) shaped like these shown on the right.

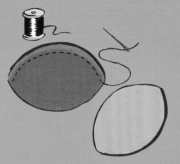

2 Sew the four pieces together, using tiny, close stitches. Leave a gap at one end in the last piece.

3 Turn the ball inside out and fill it with rice. Sew up the gap with tiny, close stitches. Make two more balls in the same way.

4 Now try to juggle! Starting with two balls in one hand and one ball in the other, throw and catch the balls, one after the other, keeping at least one ball in the air at all times.

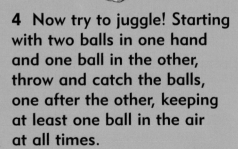

Tom is pretending to be a minstrel playing the lute.

A rotten punishment

In the market square, there's usually someone locked in the pillory. This is how people are punished for doing something wrong, such as fighting or cheating. To make the punishment worse, passers-by throw rotten vegetables at them.

This girl was caught stealing a ribbon. She'll stay in the pillory until the end of the day.

Music and dancing

Often, there are musicians at the market. There are bagpipers who play lively music for dancing. There are also minstrels who sing songs while playing a stringed instrument called a lute.

21

What we believe

One day, I'd like to go on a pilgrimage to show God that I'm a good Christian. Some people, called monks and nuns, spend their whole lives serving God. Some spend many hours copying holy books and decorating them with shining, or illuminated, letters.

I'm dressed as a pilgrim, with a wide brimmed hat and a walking stick.

Going to church

On Sunday mornings and holy days, all the people in my village go to church. We don't understand all of the service, because the priest says some of it in a language called Latin. But he also talks in English, telling us stories from the Bible that show us how to be good Christians.

Going on a pilgrimage

Sometimes we see pilgrims traveling through the forest near our village. They are going on a special religious journey to a holy place called a shrine, where they will pray. Usually pilgrims travel on foot, carrying hardly any money or baggage. Our priest says that all good Christians should try to go on a pilgrimage.

Each shrine has its own special symbol. Pilgrims visiting the shrine collect a badge showing the shrine's symbol.

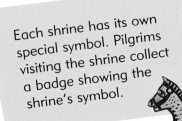

In your time...
Pilgrim badges were popular in the Middle Ages. Today, people still bring back souvenirs to remind them of places they have visited.

Let's draw an illuminated letter

Find two pieces of paper; a pencil; gold, red, and blue paint; a paintbrush; and glue.

1 First cut a small square out of one piece of paper. Then, draw a letter on the paper square and draw patterns around the letter.

2 Now paint the letter. Remember to let each color dry before painting another color.

3 Glue your illuminated letter to the other sheet of paper. Use it as the first letter of a poem, a story, or some other piece of writing.

Monks and nuns

As well as studying and copying holy books, monks and nuns have to pray at church up to eight times a day, sometimes in the middle of the night. They also farm the land, growing all their own food. Many of them give away food to people who are poor and hungry.

A monk wears a long, loose robe called a habit. Its color shows which brotherhood of monks he belongs to.

Illuminated letters are usually the first letter on a page. They're called illuminated because they are painted gold and other bright, shining colors.

Hardly anyone in my village can read or write. Villeins like me don't go to school. We learn about work from the people around us, and we learn about God from the priest or by looking at pictures in our church.

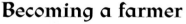

Our church has a window with pictures made of colored, or stained, glass. This one shows the king's crown.

Becoming a farmer

My parents and grandparents are teaching me how to be a farmer. I'm learning how to find out what the weather is going to be like and how to cure sick animals. Girls are taught these things too. They also learn to cook, spin, weave, and sew.

Let's make a stained-glass window

★ Adult help needed

Find black construction paper, a pencil, utility knife, colored tissue paper, scisso glue, and tape.

1 Draw the shape of the window on the construction paper. Ask an adult to cut out the shape of the window with a utility knife.

2 Cut pieces of tissue paper to fit over the cut-out shapes. On one side of the window, glue around the edge of each shape and stick on the tissue paper. When you have finished, tape your paper window to a real window so that the light shines through it.

Isobel is using herbs to make a headache cure. She's written down the recipe on a piece of parchment.

Learning to keep house

Isobel's family is rich, so she is learning many different things. Her father has taught her to read and write. She's also learning to add so that she can do the household accounts when she is married and running a house of her own. She must know how to embroider and how to make herbal remedies too.

Going to school

Rich people often pay a priest to teach their children to read and write. Some children go to a school run by a church or by a monastery, where monks live and work. Most of the pupils at these schools are boys. They learn to read and write and to speak Latin. Their teachers often beat them when they get their lessons wrong. I'm glad I don't have to go to school!

In your time...
There are still some schools today that are run by churches. Some of them have been around since the Middle Ages.

BILLINGS COUNTY PUBLIC SCHOOL
Box 307
Medora, North Dakota 58645

25

Father, Tom, and I have traveled to Westminster, to the west of London to see a great new church being built. When Tom is older, he wants to work here as a laborer. We can already see the building taking shape. It has high, arched windows and strange, carved heads called gargoyles.

Tom and I try lifting this heavy stone. It has a gargoyle on it.

All kinds of workers

There is a big team of men working on the building. Laborers are unskilled workers who do the heavy lifting jobs. Above them are skilled workers called journeymen. These include masons, who carve stone, and carpenters. In charge of everything, there is a master mason. He designed the new church and sometimes does the difficult carving jobs.

These are some of the tools a mason uses.

Let's make a gargoyle

Find thick cardboard, a pencil, and self-hardening clay.

1 Draw a gargoyle face on the cardboard.

2 Gradually build up the face of the gargoyle using pieces of clay.

3 Use your pencil to make a face on your gargoyle and to make a hole in the mouth. Let it dry, then slide the gargoyle off the cardboard.

Apprentices

People who are learning a trade, such as carpentry or masonry, are called apprentices. Villeins aren't usually allowed to learn a trade, but if a villein shows that he has a talent for a craft, he may ask his lord to free him so he can become an apprentice. Tom wants our lord to free him so he can become a mason.

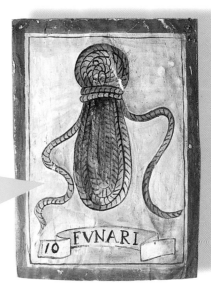

Every trade has its own special sign. This is the ropemaker's sign.

Joining a guild

Children can be apprentices when they reach twelve years of age. They have to work for a master or mistress for seven years to learn their trade. Many trades are looked after by societies called guilds. To be a tailor or a goldsmith, for example, you must belong to a guild.

You will find gargoyles like this one on church roofs. They act as water spouts, carrying rain water away through the holes in their mouths.

Our great city

On our trip, Father, Tom, and I looked at the sights of London, the biggest city in England. Father had saved up enough money to buy himself a pair of boots. He also bought Mother this pottery jug, which came all the way from France.

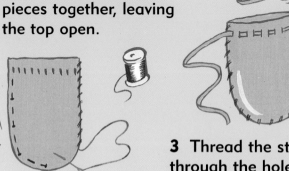

After Father bought the jug, he put his change away safely in his purse. He says that London is full of thieves!

Sights to see

The city of London is protected on three sides by a high stone wall and by the River Thames on the fourth side. A big castle, called the Tower, is in the eastern part of the city, and St. Paul's cathedral lies in the west. The most amazing sight is London Bridge, which crosses the river. It has houses built all along it.

Crowds of people

I'd never seen such crowds of people before, all forcing their way down the narrow streets. To save space, people in London build houses with two or even three floors. Some new houses have upper floors that stick out over the street.

Let's make a purse

Find felt, scissors, pins, and a needle and thread.

1 Cut out the shapes shown below from the felt so they measure 6 inches x 8 inches (15 cm x 20 cm). Snip 10 holes in the top of each shape. Now, cut out a long, thin strip of felt.

2 Pin and then sew the pieces together, leaving the top open.

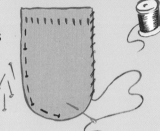

3 Thread the strip through the holes in the top of the purse and tie the two ends together.

We bought Father's boots from this shop. He liked the blue goatskin leather best, but it cost too much money!

Going shopping

Different areas of London are used by different traders. One street has only butchers' shops. Another is full of bakeries. We saw streets of goldsmiths, fish dealers, and leatherworkers. I was amazed at the number of shops and things to buy. But, like Father, I was glad to return home to my peaceful village.

In your time...
Many London streets are still named after the traders who used them in the Middle Ages. You can find Goldsmith's Row, Bread Street, Milk Street, and Ironmonger Lane.

The kitchen knight

When Isobel was at the lord's castle, she heard a minstrel telling the story of a brave man called Gareth. When she got home, she told Tom and me the tale.

King Arthur's feast

Many years ago, there was a great feast at the castle of King Arthur, ruler of England. It was the custom at a feast for the king to grant any favor that a stranger asked of him, so Arthur was not surprised when a young man called Gareth approached the throne.

Gareth said: "Sir, the favor I ask is that you give me food, drink, and shelter for one year. At the end of that time, you must grant me two more favors." King Arthur agreed and asked one of his knights, Sir Kay, to look after Gareth. Sir Kay didn't like Gareth. He thought a truly brave man would have asked for armor and a horse. So, he sent Gareth to help in the kitchens. For a year, Gareth worked hard, peeling vegetables and scrubbing floors.

The lady Linnet

A year later, King Arthur was holding another feast, when a lady arrived and asked to speak to the king. "My name is Linnet," she said, "and I need a brave knight to rescue my sister from the wicked Red Knight."

Gareth had been listening from the back of the hall and he now stepped forward from among the servants. He said to the king, "Sir, I have been here a year and I would like to ask you for my other two favors. First, make me a knight. Then, let me rescue the lady."

To Linnet's horror, the king agreed. She wanted a real knight, not a boy who worked in the kitchen!

30

Linnet stormed out of the castle, but Gareth soon caught up with her, carrying a huge sword. "What do you want, kitchen boy?" she said crossly. "I'm going to rescue your sister," he said politely.

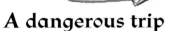

A dangerous trip

Linnet went on her way, with Gareth walking behind her. Before long, they came across a knight in black armor. "Surrender or fight!" he shouted. "He's just a kitchen boy," Linnet said. "He can't fight you." But Gareth drew his sword and attacked. Soon, the Black Knight was begging for mercy. Gareth spared him, but took his weapons and his horse. As Linnet and Gareth went on their way, they met other knights who challenged them to fight. Each knight was stronger than the last, but brave Gareth beat them all.

The Red Knight

Eventually, they arrived at the Red Knight's castle. Gareth had no time to prepare when the Red Knight suddenly galloped out of the gate with his lance raised. He hit Gareth so hard that both he and Gareth fell off their horses. They struggled to their feet and drew their swords. They fought for hours. First, one seemed to be winning, then the other. Finally, Gareth managed to seize the Red Knight's sword and had the wicked knight at his mercy.

Gareth spared the Red Knight on condition that he let Linnet's sister go. Now that Gareth had proved his courage, Linnet was ashamed of the way she had treated him. But Gareth forgave her, because after all their adventures, he loved her very much. When they returned to King Arthur's court, another great feast was held. This time it was to celebrate the marriage of Gareth and Linnet.

31

Robin's world

Robin lived over 700 years ago, but today we know a lot about his world. History detectives, called archaeologists, can piece together the story of Robin's life from such clues as pottery, jewelry, and even clothes left behind by people of the Middle Ages. Many of these things are dug out of the ground from old piles of trash.

Castles and cathedrals

Many castles and cathedrals built during the Middle Ages are still standing today in England and the rest of Europe. In some cities, people still live and work in wooden buildings that date from Robin's time.

Medieval writings

During the Middle Ages, people who owned land, such as the lords and the people of the Church, kept very good records. These records tell us which crops were planted, how much people were paid, and what crimes were committed.

Pictures and signs, such as this guild badge, help us find out about life in the Middle Ages.

Index

The words in **bold** are things that you can make.